RISING UP

Rising Up

IAN M WELLER

Ian Weller Inc

Forward

This memoir covers events from my Educational diagnosis of Asperger's Syndrome in 4th grade to near present day. It covers my struggles of being fueled by anger and rage through my long fight to find inner peace and purpose, to finding the light and gaining freedom from my darker motives. Writing this memoir wasn't easy.

This book was not written because I wanted to write it personally. I wrote this memoir at the request of the founder of Northern Michigan Autism Association, Mike Atchison. It has taken longer than I think he may have hoped. My personal hope for this book is to give some insight to the mind of one on the autism spectrum and give hope to other people, on the spectrum or family/supporters of those on the spectrum . The doctors that gave me a medical diagnosis of autism spectrum disorder when I was two years old told my parents I wouldn't graduate high school, let alone make it through middle school. I have proved them wrong along with any other skeptics I had while going through the public school system of Northern Michigan.

Also I hope by knowing my story, others can potentially avoid walking a similar dark path I have walked. As you read, you will see I didn't have an easy road to walk. I nearly carved my way through the struggles of life. My story is partially a cautionary tale for most and a story of redemption and freedom for those who are on a similar dark path. Overall I just want this book to give people hope.

Chapter 1

The year was 1998 and I just started 4th grade. I was in a meeting with a group of people. Unknown to me at the time it was a school examination. My father was there, and some of the staff from the elementary school I attended. We sat at a round table and the mediator of this meeting was a psychiatric therapist named Dr. O.

I answered some questions and was excused to go to the corner to play my Gameboy. I wasn't paying attention to what they were saying. I was too immersed in my game. Eventually I was called back into the group. I paused my game and returned to the table. Everyone was looking at me. I was oblivious to what was going on at the time.

Dr. O looked me in the eye and said, "You have Asperger's Syndrome." I had no idea what she meant at that time. Now, I realize, it was the signal that my life was soon to become more challenging.

I was naive then. Academically bright, but very naive. I didn't understand anything of what was going on around me. From that year when I entered fourth grade to the elementary school graduation at the end of fifth grade, I knew very little of anything outside of what was taught in school at the time. Everything I knew at the time was either taught to me by my parents or teachers I had. There was the occasional insight that came in from a place I can't recall.

After going through half of sixth grade, things started to change for me. My perspective changed; I matured beyond my age in understanding. Then the hard part began. The first school year of the new millennium, fall 2001, was when I started to pay a price for receiving my mental maturity at least five years before everyone else my age.

September 11th was a dark day for the United States of America. I was sitting in my seventh grade history class. My middle school principal, Mr. H, poked his head in the room and said, "We've been attacked." Before I could say anything, he was gone. I didn't know what happened until I got home and my family talked about it.

The next day I was in my home room when Principle H activated the intercom system.

"Attention students, this morning we will be walking to the funeral home to attend a ceremony for those who died during the attack yesterday. Get your coats."

I stood from my desk and walked to the door. I didn't understand much about the attack then. I didn't know the situation, or how many lives were lost that day.

I quickly opened my locker, put my coat on, and was the first to walk out the middle school doors with the rest of the students and staff several feet behind me. Most of the students took their time socializing among other things. I was task oriented, as I interpreted the announcement was "Get your coat, then get to the funeral home". Everything was black and white to me. Striding briskly, I walked down Mason Street heading toward Downtown Charlevoix which was the direction of the funeral home from the middle school at that time.

As the lawn came into view, I saw a small group of people there already along with two uniformed military personnel raising the flag to the top of the flagpole, then lowering it to half-mast. Behind me I heard the chatter of the other students. I took my place on the lawn around the flagpole.

Even though I didn't understand it all, I knew how ceremonies like this worked. You bowed your head and stayed silent unless you were given permission to talk. That was the way I understood it. That was the way I was taught. I have been to a couple funerals before that day. My parents told me to be quiet at such ceremonies. Knowing this, I stood silent as others gathered around the flagpole.

Part way through the ceremony, we were asked for a moment of silence. As the moment started, I heard two people jabbering and being disrespectful, desecrating this moment of silence. I turned toward the direction of the conversation. I shouldn't have been surprised. The two who were talking were two I usually had to tolerate. My anger built up inside, I wanted to do something, but I couldn't. If I did do something, it would have been more disrespectful than what they were doing now. The rest of the ceremony was uneventful. When the ceremony was over, it was back to the middle school. I slipped my way through the crowd of people as they were disbanding. I eventually got to the front of the crowd heading to the middle school and picked up to my usual brisk stride.

As for the two I had to tolerate, they were part of a group of three that picked on me. They saw me as entertainment, making fun of my interests with lies, bullshit, and occasionally tried to make a point that my interests were nothing. They knew it would anger me, and they used that anger as entertainment. When I started to lash out, they ran like a small mouse being chased by a mean cat. It was a game to them, for when I chased one and almost have them in my grasp, another would send an insult and I would focus on the other one. They did this until I was exhausted or recess was over.

It is sad when the people your age you call 'friends' sometimes do the same thing. They would occasionally make fun of me, but the difference is they knew when to stop. I forgave my friends mainly because no one else back then near my age would even support me when I needed it. I admit I have strange taste in people.

My friends and I became distant as time went by. They decided to experience a darker path of drugs, alcohol, and other stupidity, while I stayed on the path I've been on. I was what many would call a 'straight arrow.' I would prefer the term 'obedient dog,' because that was the way I functioned. If those whom I viewed as my superiors asked me to do something, I did it. If I was told to follow instructions, I followed them to the letter.

Unknown to me, a darker path of a different kind had developed within me. After two years of bullying, insults and small outbursts in middle school, I entered high school. To my mild surprise, the bullies disappeared. I figured I had a bodyguard in my older brother, who was a Junior at the time, or else they were just bored. But the damage was done, and the seeds were sown.

As I walked into the high school on the first day of school, I constructed a mental fortress inside myself. I didn't trust anyone I didn't already know, and I didn't trust anyone who wasn't in my small circle of friends. I had the thought that my classmates hated me, thus they let me suffer mentally at the hands of bullies.

As a result, I quietly hated them as well.

I had a thirst for revenge. An eye for an eye was demanded from my point of view. I didn't act on that thirst, for all I could do at the time was plan. I kept this dark side of me hidden as much as I could. I knew I would have to wait for the right time to strike if I *was* to strike.

The part that may seem scary, or should be scary, is that I didn't want to get revenge by hurting them, I wanted them dead. My classmates left me to die, or hoped I would commit suicide so they wouldn't have blood on their hands. This was just pure theory, mind you. I had no evidence, just a hunch. Thus I would take it a step further, do what they could not. These thoughts circled in my head, but I never acted on them. The whole time I was in high school, my acts of kindness to my classmates were nothing more than mass deception. When I would help my classmates with favors was just a way to get them to lower their guard. So when I would strike, they would be petrified and dumbfounded at the same time.

Whenever I did blade practice, a practice of swordsmanship, with a stick, some of them saw me practicing, they had no idea the imaginary foes I was cutting down was them. The practice was me getting the revenge I desired. The irony is that they sometimes cheered me on. If they knew the truth of who I was fighting in those practices, I'm certain they wouldn't be cheering. They would be nervous or uneasy when I was around.

Chapter 2

The year is 2004. It's fall, I'm sitting in 10th grade biology class and I had completed my in class assignment early. I went into the small lab between the rooms of the two biology teachers. There was a white board on one of the walls with dry erase markers. On that surface I wrote my first vent poem. It was titled "I Stand Alone". I made a mistake: I put 'by' with my last name on it. I hoped that if anyone saw it they may think it was my brother and not me.

It didn't work that way at all. As soon as I got home from school and my dad got home from work as well. He confronted me about it. Apparently someone saw the poem and drew the attention of the entire school staff. They put me at the top of the suspect list and notified my father. In the kitchen, he proceeded to yell at me in a tone I never heard before. I ended up becoming a sobbing ball on the floor when it was over. The main reason, the only reason I can think of, was I didn't have the willpower to fight back against my own parents at that time in my life.

My high school counselor, Mr. P, called me in to talk about it the next morning. He was far more light hearted about it than my dad was the evening before. He told me every staff member in the school looked at it. They admitted it was well written even though the content was questionable as he put it. He gave me the option of using the computers in the counseling center to write out the poems. I don't remember all of it, but I rewrote it. I called it the original one when I was done on the high school computer. I probably changed the entire thing. It had the same song chorus idea in it. But I think it was missing something from it. Now that I think about it I left out an old Latin proverb: "if you want peace, prepare for war". That proverb is probably what made it get so much attention. Here is the original rewrite of the poem that started it all, I Stand Alone:

I Stand Alone (2004)

I stand alone, 'tis my life to stand alone.
I stand alone where I am in this world.
I stand alone in my situation.
None can help me with my pain.
I stand for justice and virtue.
I will die before these concepts do.
I stand alone, 'tis my life to stand alone.
One of these days all hell will be raised.
I will be there to fight it, alone.
For none will stand by my side.
I only see things black and white.
Light and Dark.
For this I am exiled from the rest of my age group.
I stand alone, and I shall forever stand alone.
'Tis my life to be alone.
Now let me die.

Yes, that was the format I used at the time in high school because I didn't know anything about poetry and stanzas at the time. It was title and statement after statement block poetry. It wasn't anything fancy but it was the thoughts that I had bottled up and sprayed on to a surface that could have writing on it. The thing that may sound sad is all of the poems I wrote in high school were the same format, different lengths and different subjects, and always centered aligned. To my understanding now it's pure amateur format. If an image is included it can be justified.

As you could tell from the content and feeling in the poem, I felt alone. I was the outcast everyone ignored. Ironically, I was in that role because I put myself there.

Another thing that made me feel alone, there were two other people in my year class that shared my name. A total of three people, including me, named "Ian". It gets old, annoying, and aggravating very fast when someone says your name and after you respond they say "The other Ian". You're willing to tolerate it a few times. But months of it adds fuel to the anger fire. It burns for such a long period sustained you'd think it has an infinite supply under it.

Junior year, I was contemplating suicide. I was growing tired of holding all the anger and rage inside to protect others. Even though most of those people I felt at the time weren't worth protecting. It was the same thing over and over again. I felt worthless, and like I didn't belong in this world. I felt I had more in common with the honored dead than the current people around me.   When I'd think about it at home, the farthest I would ever go is grabbing a large kitchen knife. I would always look at the knife and think to myself "Is this the right choice?". Questions flooded into my mind. "What would happen to my family?", "What would happen to those I cared about?", and so on. As those questions circled in my head, I always put the knife back. No one knew about these thoughts.

I thought about suicide at school too. The school windows were like latch doors on rooftops. You could open them to almost a ninety degree angle. The only thing that kept from being opened too much was a screen cover over the window. Turns out the screen weren't as secure as it could've been. There were eight little tabs that held it in place.

I went to the window at the back of the classroom and slowly moved the tabs so they weren't holding the screen in place. Some of the classmates asked what I was doing. I would say "nothing" or "nothing to worry about". I told them that so they wouldn't suspect what I was doing.

The school was a two floor building. The window I was at was almost ideal for the end I sought. On the ground floor near the window I was working on was a doorway. On the other side of the doorway, there was a large concrete slab then grass. Part of the concrete slab was under the window I was working on.

The plan was straightforward; get the screen off, open the window, go out the window head first, and hopefully hit the concrete. The resulting contact would snap my neck, killing me instantly.

Of course, I didn't get past step two before my teacher noticed. "Whoa, Ian what are you doing?!" exclaimed my English teacher, Mr. C. At this point the screen was off and against a wall, while I had my hand on the handle that would open the window. "Getting a better breeze," I replied knowing it was a lie.

Everyone in the room looked at me in silence. At that moment, I felt if I fell out that window, there wouldn't be screams of shock. I was certain, if I fell out, I would hear cheers as I went down.

I changed my mind at that point. If I died then, I figured it would give them satisfaction to be rid of me. Now I think they would have wondered what drove me to do that, while they were too ignorant to understand that they, my classmates, were the reason. They left me to rot, suddenly they're in shock.

Chapter 3

Near the final quarter of that school year I made the connection to what I am. In my US History class, we had a special weekly research assignment of current events. My teacher Mr. H gave us a current event topic and we had to use a news database the school had available to find an article about that topic. It had to be dated within two weeks of the due date otherwise it didn't count.

Our last research assignment was a 'wild card' assignment. We chose a topic in recent publication and presented it. I had a Newsweek magazine at home that had Autism as the cover story. I thought, 'may as well take a look'. Its issue date was the same week as the wild card project, so I thought that might be useful. As I read this article, it talked about the ends of the autism spectrum. At the high functioning end was something I recognized. At the high functioning end of the spectrum was a diagnosis of Asperger's Syndrome.

My diagnosis I was told years before was part of the autism spectrum. It wasn't disheartening. It was more like an epiphany that brought relief. I finally understood why I was so different from everyone else.

I was going to reveal my epiphany to my history class, but Mr. H had other ideas. Instead of the normal research teams getting together to discuss findings we just turned in all the research we did. I don't remember why it was important at the time, I just thought it was.

Also, near the end of the school year in my English class, we were required to submit a creative writing sample. In my case, I submitted two short poems that were dark, but it may have opened the eyes of my classmates a little bit.

The reason I say that is the fact they were more accepting and inviting than the past several years combined. It may seem like a big improvement, but it was more like a minimal to average improvement. Another thing may have been that I said in the last class before the end of semester exams, I told my classmates in my English class that I had Autism. It may have been a revelation for them when they both heard that and read the poems I submitted.

The poems I submitted were titled "Cursed" and "I am". Here are the poems in stanza format, rather than the bulk block they were in originally:

Curse

I bear something that is to be my end.

This burden is a gift that gives me life.
It is also a curse that tears me apart.

I guess it may be worth the pain of isolation.
Look where I am,
I am in one physical piece and I have made good choices
But all around me are people making bad choices

My curse is my darkness
My anger, my frustration against people

Will I be free from my darkness?

Will I be free from pain?

I am

Every day I am reminded what I really am.
Everything I see reminds me of what I really am.
The people around me, though they do not speak,
their actions tell me what I really am.

They see me as a spirit that walks around the halls of
this school.
Only the adults see me as a whole.
The students rarely see me at all.

They will never know because they will never under-
stand.
They will never understand in this state of mind.

I am alone in a world of chaos.
Darkness is all around me.
What should I do?

Chapter 4

The summer between Junior and Senior year, I tried out for the high school football team. I still wanted to die, but I decided I wouldn't commit suicide. If I was to die, I would die by carelessness on my part, not by a weapon in my hand. Using a weapon to kill yourself is a coward's way to die. And I refused to die like a coward. The football team would allow me to die by overexertion from the workouts or, since I lacked being physically prepared, I hoped a good hard hit would ultimately do me in.

It didn't work out as planned. I was unable to exhaust myself and I barely got to play. The thoughts of suicide went to the back burner as the senior year went on.

The football season went rather well for the team. Seven or eight wins and one loss in the regular season. We qualified for the state postseason, and upon hearing the schedule of the game tournament system I got a little worried.

My older brother was going to college in Florida. My family and I were under obligations to go to Florida and spend Thanksgiving with him. If we made it to the state finals, we would have to play on Thanksgiving Day. Now my dilemma, if we got that far I would have to choose between my family and the team. The guys were good and I already knew I wouldn't be needed, but I had to be there to support them. That was one of the main rules about being on the team. Even if you didn't play, you had to be there to support the team. My parents said they would worry about it when the time came. I had to have faith things would work out for the best.

We didn't make it past Regionals. We did our best, but our best wasn't enough. My teammates on the sidelines were crying as the clock ticked down to the end, I on the other hand wasn't crying, I was furious.

At the time whenever my side or myself was losing in a game, I was getting wound up and ready to blow. That was how I was for a long time. After the game was over, we did the usual after game stretches. Everyone around me was crying, me, I was waiting to let out all this anger inside. I got my chance. We went into the locker building and as I entered, I took off my helmet and hurled it at a mirror next to the locker room entrance. It already had a crack in it, and when my helmet hit the mirror, the crack looked like a tree. Some of the guys saw me throw it and had this "Oh shit" look of shock on their face. I told the coaches after I got changed. Surprisingly, they shrugged their shoulders and said "Don't worry about it". It didn't mean that much, other than I didn't have to pay to replace the mirror.

After football was over with Thanksgiving break came the next entertaining senior event that all the school was involved in. I personally called it "The Egg Wars". The seniors taking Sociology would end up in the family unit and be given a part-ner or able to do the project on their own. Those who chose to work alone were given a random scenario by the teacher. She was notorious for making these scenarios as hard as possible for the loners. At least with a partner you got to choose what you had to start with.

The partner pairings were done at random for my class. The guys in the class were to pick a girl's name out of a goldfish bowl and ask if they would like to be their partner. Eventually my turn came up. Like the other guys I put my hand in and pulled out a slip of paper with a name. I saw the name and shrugged my shoulders. I moved my thumb a little bit to realize I accidently took two names instead of one. I said out loud "You gotta be kidding. I can't support two families". The teacher came up and told me to ask both of them. I was thinking to myself, "I'm going to be taking a lot of shit for this". I walk up to my first choice of the two names. Her name was H. I didn't even ask. I showed her the slip of paper with her name on it. She agreed to be my partner and I turned and said the name of the second person I drew. Lucky for me she said "I was thinking of doing this alone". I was grateful.

After that H and I worked together to plan the career paths and number of kids. Here is where the name of the event comes in. Our 'kids' were special wrapped and marked eggs. We had to return them the exact way we received them. The job of the rest of the school was to abduct the eggs and take them to Mrs. S so she could ransom them.

We decided to have two kids, hence two eggs. I don't remember how H carried her egg around school, but I had mine in a big canister filled with cotton balls and a leashed lid. I had the leash going through a belt loop hole in my pants. In the job category, H chose to be a stay at home mom, and I somehow was a high paid writer. Actually, I chose 'writer' and the teacher gave me a spending limit of $500,000 a year. I ended up doing all the numbers. I calculated expenses for everything that I could access and chose a house that would be a family home. H and I agreed on a car, but not on a house yet. I found two houses that would work. I did the financial math for both of them. For home insurance costs I just picked a number that would be considered reasonable, which was about $200 a month. I waited for the next class to talk to H about which house she would prefer.

When the class began, Mrs. S declared "Twist of Fate". She went on to explain what it meant. Before getting with our partners, one from each partnership had to come up (presumably the husband) and draw a fate slip that would impact you in some way. I got up when it was my turn and drew a slip. I look at the slip and it read in these terms. "Your house caught on fire and it burned to the ground".

"Oh shit," I thought. "H is not going to be happy."

I then went over to H and showed her the pictures of the two houses. I kept my mouth shut about the fate slip and asked "Which one do you like?" while at the back of my mind, it was more like "What's going to die?". She chose the nicer looking one of the two. Then I was forced to show her the fate slip. Her eyes widened and jaw dropped with shock.

"What do we do?" H asked.

"Give me some time, I got to ask some questions," I replied. I spent some time talking with Mrs. S on how much would a premium like the one I chose would cover, while everyone else was in a nearby computer lab working on numbers and their final paper for the project. She said "All of it. All you have to do is add some expenses for replacement gifts and clothes."

I literally started to give the "eureka" laugh and continued to laugh as I went to tell H the surprising news. When I told her, her eyes lit up and her jaw dropped with a smile forming on her face. "I'll work on the new numbers," I said. "At least we aren't living on the street."

Before the next class started the next week, I got to class early as usual and Mrs. S told me H was bragging on how I was an economic genius. I didn't believe it. I believed that everyone in my class despised me. I thought they were doing the same thing I was throughout high school. A ploy of respect and acceptance, so they would never suspect I would kill them when the time came. I assumed they were trying to lower my guard.

At the time, if what she said was true or not, I didn't care. I was too thick headed to believe someone who I felt despised me would be saying praises about me. It was also the last class before Christmas break. We turned in our eggs and our project response papers.

Christmas break came and went, and it was back to school in January. In my Advanced English class, we read some works that inspired me to write or, in the case of the book Siddhartha, had to write a poem for an assignment. The assignment poem came later. The inspired poem was caused by a short work in our textbook that had similarities to the Folk song "The Sound of Silence" by Simon & Garfunkel. I titled it 'Mistakes Go On'.

Mistakes Go On

We will always make mistakes.
It is the nature of humans.
Both those with hearts and without.

As long as darkness and light live intertwined
The unrecorded small mistakes
Will lead to bigger problems to be repeated

Humanity may never learn from its mistakes,
If all of them are not recorded.

And as long as anger and hate live
There will always be problems.

Some humans never learn.
They are too cocky
Too foolish
Too stupid to understand

But there are some
That are wise and understand

The sad truth is
They are rare.
And a few of them that come to be
Don't last that long.

Even when others come
To take their place among the wise
They cannot stand to see all that the wisest sees.

The price of wisdom at an early age
Can be madness.

I placed this and another poem I wrote that year into a poetry contest the school held for its students. The piece that helped me win wasn't 'Mistakes Go On'. 'Mistakes Go On' and the previous submissions were all dark in a sense. The piece that won was a more calming and positive work titled 'Peace'. To be honest, this piece came out of the blue. I don't remember how it got written, I just remember typing up a storm and 'poof' there it was. I printed it off and showed it to a girl I admired for a long time. She seemed mildly impressed and said it made her want to do yoga.

Peace

Peace is rare but it can be found in many places in the world.
The primary place is in nature.

The sound of mild silence and the calming wind.
The sound of Mother Nature herself.

It is a sign of tranquility.
Nature is at peace.
Peace is in the quiet places in the world.

Not places such as caves, where noise echoes.
But the forest, wilderness, or plains where noise can be made, and none will care.
Those are the places where you can find peace in both mind and body.

The places where you can find peace
Are not in a city.
Only in nature.

I entered in the contest before during my Sophomore and Junior years of high school. The contest was almost an all or nothing competition. If you participated, you got a copy of the collected submissions. If you did the cover art or won, you got something extra. Past two years, I got the participation prize. That year I won.

The rest of the school year was mostly uneventful. The only last few events of note are Senior Prom, Graduation rehearsal, and Graduation Day itself. The Prom I was tricked into participating and the Graduation events I actually wanted to take part in.

I normally didn't attend school dances. They are usually all the same, a bunch of people gathered and loud music playing. I should also note, the Senior Prom is the only school dance I ever attended. I had no desire to go because of my hatred toward my classmates.

I was tricked because I had classmates say I should go and my high school counselor said I should go and record parts of the event. My classmates I didn't take into account, but I felt I should listen to my counselor. The reason is because I was a part of the class he was teaching about broadcasting. I was under the impression no one from the class would attend and record highlights of the event. As I had my own video camera, I felt obligated to go.

The theme for that year was Hollywood. So the plan was to have a red carpet going into the venue where it was held and a bunch of people with cameras to take pictures like the paparazzi. I had no desire to walk down the red carpet. I basically said that if I did walk it, I would have the finger upside down and not look happy to be there. Thankfully there was a second way to the front door of the venue. I went up the handicap ramp to avoid the cameras.

As I approach the front door, I see a classmate of mine with one of the school cameras. At that moment I knew I was tricked. We chatted a little bit as I went inside. I got in position to get ready to film the event. The night was a bit stressful. I felt so uncomfortable a few times I needed to go outside and relax.

Part of the stress was the loud music. There is no more awkward feeling I have ever experienced than feeling the soundwaves shaking my ribcage. I couldn't even get close to the dance floor. I'd get too close to the speakers, the soundwaves would hit me and I would be forced to stagger backwards with my free hand on my chest trying to reduce the vibrations I was feeling in my ribs. Once it got to the crowning of the Prom Kings and Queens, I recorded the dimly lit dancing and left.

The following Monday I added my video footage to the rest of the collected footage of the event. After adding the footage I went through wondering if there was any footage of me. Turns out there was. It was me talking and walking in the front door. I, with no regret, deleted the footage.

During the graduation rehearsal, we were to pair up for the walk into the gym where the ceremony was taking place. I planned on walking alone. It turns out I wasn't the only one thinking of that course. The staff put their foot down on that idea as soon as they found out. They demanded we go in pairs, but a problem arose. There was an odd number of students attending the ceremony. Now they had two options, one person walks alone or one person has two partners. They decided one person would have two partners. The only reason this is brought up is because I was the one person with two partners. When the decision was announced, I thought "This is going to be embarrassing". My partners were two girls named N and H.W (not the same H that was in my Sociology class). I had a girl on each arm. I would walk into the gym like a man who managed the world's oldest profession.

Being a person who tries to follow the code of chivalry, I wasn't in favor of this plan. The code of chivalry stated, in writing I think, a man can only hold the hand of one woman at a time. It was referring to romance and love, but personally I applied it to all social situations. I knew I had to follow the plan, didn't mean I had to like it.

When the ceremony began and it came to my turn to enter the gym, I walked in with a girl on each arm. As soon as we came into view of the stands, I heard people yelling praises. "Woo ho", "Yeah man", "Way d'a go", that sort of thing were the praises. The stereotypical construction crew on lunch break when they see a very attractive woman, was the kind of things that were said when I came in and got to my seat.

After the ceremony was complete, we all went to the court-yard for the "cap throw" picture. I am the easiest person to find in the picture. I didn't want to be in the picture. I got as far from the student body as I thought was needed to get cut out of the picture. I was filled with so much anger, hatred, and other negative emotions at the time; I felt, to my year class, I should be nothing more than a memory. I got called out to get closer so I could be in the picture. I didn't have to be in the group, but I had to be in the picture.

We threw our caps and the picture was taken. As the others looked for their personalized caps, I left the courtyard. I looked for my parents with the idea of "the party's over, time to leave". I found them and did a couple quick conversations of 'congrats' and 'thank you'. I'm certain I was the first student of the graduating class to be off the campus grounds after the ceremony.

I wanted that part of my life over with and move on to the next. I had plans for the next step of my life. What my family and I had planned wasn't the same plan someone higher up had laid out for us.

Chapter 5

My family and I had a plan of moving to Florida after I graduated high school. The plan was set, everything was in place. Sadly, when one part of a train comes off the tracks, the whole train goes with it. After my father's contract with a waste management company in Northern Michigan expired, they let him go earlier than expected. Also, my mother became obligated to stay because of medical issues with her parents. We couldn't afford to own two houses. I was set to go to college in Florida. I went through orientation, I had classes set, everything was in place, except the finances that were needed were nowhere to be found.

In short, I couldn't go to my college of choice. I had to contact them and tell them I wasn't coming this semester. They did contact me again in October, saying they were preparing for me to be there for the next semester and wonder if I could make it. I was forced to tell them I couldn't. They sounded excited to have me there. It hurt me more to tell them I couldn't come and I would reapply when I had the ability to go. When things started to fall, I was doing the same thing I did every summer: working the same part time job I had since the summer of the year I turned 14 years old. But I continued to work the same kind of hours into the fall and through the winter.

When the Winter semester of colleges came around in January 2008. My parents got me to register in the local community college in the city of Petoskey. I went to North Central Michigan College to get an Associates Degree. But to be honest, my life was nothing more than a ship drifting through the ocean during that period.

I did amass a collection of poems during the time between high school graduation and the Associate Degree. I will admit a great number of those poems were very dark, also very personal. They were "train of thought" type of works.

Some of them went into what would eventually become my first self-published collection of poems. The poems ranged from "dark" to "bizarre", with the occasional "positive" note or "questioning the way the world works". Here some samples of those works. If you wish to skip ahead to the next Chapter, I won't be offended. But if you want to truly know how I felt then and try to understand, here are the sample works from the period. Turn the Page.

Pain

Why?
Why am I in so much internal pain?

What have I done to earn this pain?
I am forced to bear this pain by myself.
I am always on the brink of death,
But I do not die.

What is it that keeps me alive?
Hope,
Faith,
Heart,
or is it something I don't know?

I know I should live so I can take care of my family
Because my brother won't.
Though it appears that I make their lives complete,
Do they really need me?

The life of my first love seems complete and happy without me.
My heart aches because of it.

Some say I'm charming, and cool
But I am sure that they are just saying it to make me feel good,
Or are they telling the truth?

I guess I'll never know.
For my peers have disbanded and gone their separate ways,
While I am temporarily trapped in one place.

I am decaying inside,

Though physically I am young and strong.
What is happening within me?

Battlefield

Why is my mind a battlefield?
A battlefield where
my primitive vengeful motives
fights my reason.

I didn't start it,
but I am bound to finish it.
How can I get rid of these old feelings of vengeance for good?

The battle has raged for years.
I don't know how to end it?
Must it end in bloodshed,
or in understanding?

I don't know.
They say they were young and stupid,
for part of me, that isn't a good excuse.
I know I have had an adult mentality longer than any of them.

Therefore part of me expects that they were to be at the same level,
then and now.

I know that was wishful thinking.
This battle in my mind must end somehow.

But how is it to end,
bloodshed,
understanding,
or my end?

If I'm Worth Saving

I have fought with myself for a long time.
I feel alone.

I know many people care about me,
but they can't save me from the darkness..

If I'm worth saving,
do what you can to help.

If I'm worth saving,
help me find my way;
for I feel lost.

I know the path for my goals.
But the path that leads to spiritual growth,
I have only gone in circles.

I'm lost in a maze.
A maze where a clue is seen in the corner of your eye,
but when you turn to look at it directly,
it's gone.

Something doesn't want me to leave.
It watches me,

like a scientist observing a lab rat in a maze of walls.
I'm lost in questions and thoughts of both darkness and twilight.

If I'm worth saving,
help me find the answer to these strange riddles.

Belong

I have thought and wondered.
For years I have been searching.

We all have a place in this world,
whether it be a small task or something more.
Many people wonder this same question I ask myself.
"Where do I belong?"

This question applies to all aspects of life.
Do I belong in my hometown?
Am I meant for great things?
Or am I to be a pawn for the success of another?

These questions haunt me,
and I know they haunt others as well.

What are we meant to do?
Where do we belong?

Impossible Love

Love,
it's such an easy concept.
Almost anyone can find love.

Me,
I think I am one of those people who can fall in love,
but not be able to be loved.

Who would fall in love with me?

I have things to offer,
but they would have the burden by my unstable mind.

Real love is impossible for me.
Once they find out about my unstable mind,
they will leave me.

And the true test of my willpower will begin.
The struggle to keep things together,
while my spirit and heart are shattered.

To keep things together means life.
To have things fall apart completely,
means death.

Chapter 6

2010 brought a new chapter in my life: Central Michigan University. I had some encounters there that helped me in the long run. I was trying to go for the educator path. The first semester with the education major didn't go well.

The Intro to Education class didn't work out because I still had lingering scars affecting my judgment. The old fashion authoritarian approach to a classroom setting was no longer favorable in the schools today. That was the approach I was planning. I wanted to be able to pass on knowledge while also being a figure of authority. One of my professors gave me a verbal slap in the face when she told me being an educator is likely not a good fit for me. She was probably right at the time. I wanted to be the kind of teacher I grew up with that bluntly said "You don't have to like it, but you have to do the work."

I took part in some groups and activities. I didn't know anyone there and I knew I needed a support network there to be able to have a chance. There was a poetry slam group called Word Hammer at CMU at the time. When I saw it I thought "A poetry group; that may be a good fit for me." I didn't know what a Poetry Slam was. I found out the hard way it was reciting poems you write and adding performance to the recital in front of a crowd. I wasn't that good at performance, let alone remembering my works word for word off the top of my head. Doing this in front of an auditorium full of students, didn't make it any easier. My writing was good, but presenting before a crowd was a new experience to me. The first few slams I took part in were likely terrible for me because I didn't know my work off the top of my head and I had no idea of what I was doing.

I made a friend by getting into a card game I used to play back in Charlevoix with my friends. They lost interest and I had no one to play with. I had the cards, but it was so long ago I didn't know some of the new rules and changes that have come about. The first night of playing the card game again was a disaster. Everyone there were at a more competitive state than I was. I was playing people that played at renowned invite-only events. The shining highlight of this humbling experience was that I made a friend that helped me get back into it and has been on my side ever since.

He and I had a few adventures together. One eventually made it into poetry form. It was the weekend before Halloween; most of the students were dressed up, getting ready to party. My friend and I weren't taking part in the Halloween spirit. The reason, mostly because I felt I was too old to take part in the costume dress up. After going to the college store in my dorm complex for some snacks and drinks I didn't have, we headed back to the elevators that went to my dorm room. We met a guy who was drunk and dressed up with sealed condom packages. Here's the poem form of the event:

Wasted Trojan

Three days from Halloween
In a dorm complex at CMU.
I'm walking on the first floor
To my hall in the complex.

To set the scene

*I'm casually dressed
In a long sleeve t-shirt
Blue jeans and sneakers.*

*My friend,
Who is walking next to me
Has a blue t-shirt with
A picture of Sonic's head in the middle
Blue jeans and tennis shoes.*

*We approach the elevators
and in front of them
are some students laughing*

*The leader of the group
Has a foam Roman helmet on.
A cape that was a CMU banner.
Flip flops, shorts, as well as
A strap from his left shoulder
To the right side of his waist
And a strap dress
All the straps are different
condom packs taped together.*

*He turned to look at us
With this idiot grin on his face;
Indicating he's obviously wasted.*

*He points at my friend
And says
"Hey man, you're Sonic."*

Points at me

And says
"I don't know what you're supposed to be
But you scare the shit out of me."

If there was no background noise
You could hear a pin drop.

I did the right thing.
I keep my mouth shut
And glared at him.

After thirty seconds
Of glaring silence
The elevator dings, doors open,
And the group got in.

What I could've done;
Was grab the knot of the cape
With my right hand
And yanked him toward me
With all the strength in my right arm
Glare into his eyes
And said
"I'm on edge.
And when I'm on edge
I occasionally get the thirst for blood.
I'm thinking about using yours to satisfy it."

Just then, elevator doors would open,
I'd let him go
He and his group would get on the elevator.

If I was lucky
and performed the intimidation right

as the doors closed
I would hear someone in it say
"Man did you shit yourself?"

The only mildly entertaining part to this story is after the drunk and his friends got on the elevator, some girls came by. My friend told them what we just saw. They replied "Oh, we missed him". I thought to myself, "The only way you would be seeing him right now is if I was on top of him trying to rip his throat out". Even if I wanted to, I couldn't. Besides eye witness testimonies, there were at least three cameras that would have got the whole thing on film. There was no way I could lash out and walk away without consequences.

The end of CMU was disastrous, I did very poorly in academics which resulted in being removed from enrollment. It was a massive leap from what I knew and I didn't have the support network or people to keep me on track. The first semester was a struggle to keep things together between long run research project with a very vague topic and trying to be somewhat social. The last straw was failing one course I could have dropped. I thought I needed to maintain a certain amount of credit classes to stay in the dorms, when I found out I could drop, it was too late. In the end, I got what I needed most from there, a friend who would have my back no matter the distance.

Chapter 7

Being embarrassed by the CMU experience and being forced to return home with my tail between my legs would be the summary of the following summer. When I got back I ended up doing what I did every summer. The only positive is when fall came around I re-enrolled in North Central Michigan College and finished up getting an associate degree and training for my next backup profession.

I wanted to be a writer since I started college, but my family told me, "Get a backup plan before going after your dreams." With the educator plan down the drain, I looked to the internet. North Central Michigan College offered a program in New Media which covered video editing and internet web development. I did some internet work at CMU as part of the initial educator program. It was the only class I got a good grade in that first semester.

The classes for that were straight forward enough for me to get into and pass with some ease. I passed the classes and got an Associate's degree and a Certificate in New Media. Now came the hard part, putting the new skill-set into use. There weren't many places in Northern Michigan that were looking for a rookie website builder. Especially when I learned, after I got employed, most of what I learned was outdated and just scratching the surface of a much bigger world.

In the time between graduation and becoming employed, I developed a draft of my first poetry collection. It was meant to be a Christmas gift idea for my family. The first draft included all the poems shown up to this point and more. When I asked for someone to review it, the response was not what I was expecting: There were some grammar errors, but the real problem was that it was too dark. The person who reviewed it said "After reading it, I look at the gun on the wall". It was the opinion of just one person, but it was an opinion I valued because it was an outsider perspective. Even my own mother who got a copy of the first draft said it made her sad.

I then began the mass weeding of poems in the first collection to make it more reader friendly. I went through each poem. When I came across something that could be taken out, I said to myself "Too dark", "Too personal", or "Too bizarre". I ended up whittling it down to less than fifty pages of content. After I got the cover design done, I noticed it was very thin. At least what I lacked for in quantity, I made up for in quality. When I tried to have the first copies printed, the minimal amount of printable copies was twenty five. I needed three or four copies for gifts, so I had about twenty two copies to do something with.

After the gifting, my family said, "Try selling them to bookstores". I did get a few compensation contracts set up with a couple local bookstores. Also, my mother kept a few copies to sell off record and gave me the money she made. My parents were proud and excited that I managed to self publish a book on my own. But I didn't show much enthusiasm as they did. To be honest I shrugged my shoulders and was trying to find my place again.

Something happened next that I didn't expect. The first poetry collection sold. I personally don't know how, but I got a phone call from a book store telling me they wanted more copies. I gave the book store five to start and they were sold out in a week. The book store was in my hometown of Charlevoix, Michigan. This recurred multiple times to the point where I had to order more books to be printed. I ended up ordering seventy five more copies to make sure I kept up with demand.

The demand for the poetry book subsided as summer ended and winter set in. By winter, I was also employed in Petoskey Michigan at an internet marketing group by then as well. I found something online when I was looking for another way to occupy my time. I found an autism support group called Northern Michigan Autism Association. I first saw it as a marketing opportunity to sell more of the books. After a few meetings, I stopped bringing the books. Besides the fact they weren't selling very well at the time, I found I am better as a passive member. The group was made of parents who all had children on the autism spectrum. I felt a little out of place at first, but I realized I should give these parents, who are looking for resources to help their children, something to look forward to. Autism was shown in a negative light and there were very few open resources to parents who didn't know where to look in northern Michigan.

I wasn't the perfect example, but I was something they could see and look forward to. For those parents that was enough. I ended up getting the title of "the shining example of what one on the spectrum can be". To this day, it stuck.

I don't mind the title that much. The greatest positive about this "shining example" is that I give a sense of hope to people. I may not be a celebrity or influencing the masses, but I am doing something right.

After becoming a mascot for the group in a sense, I started to work on a second collection of poems. These were newer poems that gave a feeling of support and more uplifting feel than the previous collection. It was about the same size as the previous collection. Here are a few sample poems from it.

Do You Know

Do you know
what Autism is?

Do you know
it affects 1 in 54
children born in the US.

Do you know
that when a child
is diagnosed with Autism,
a special needs family is made.

If one person has Autism
the whole family is
part of the Autism community.

Most families are devastated
when they get the diagnosis.
They lose hope when hope can be found.

Allow me to help you
on your journey of
overcoming this challenge
known as Autism

Most know nothing,

so they do nothing.
The more involved you are
the easier the process will be.

Continue on,
and be strengthened by my words.

Listen to what an
Autism success story has to say.

Be Proud

My brothers and sisters
of situation.
I know it's hard.
What I'm about to ask
may seem too much.

Be Proud,
Proud of who you are.

If someone
calls you inferior,
they don't know anything.

They don't know you,
You may have weak points,
but you also have strengths

If you are doing
the best you can,

giving it your all.

No matter the outcome,
Be proud of yourself.

Autism comes with challenges.
If you are doing your best
and refuse to give up,
That's something
to be proud of.

All we can do
is the best we can.

If you are doing your best,
you and your family
should be proud.

Don't

Listen to me.

My autistic
brothers and sisters,
listen to what I have
to say.

Don't kneel
to the elites
that don't understand.

*Only bow
as a polite courtesy,
depending on culture.*

*In the U.S.
don't bow,
kneel,
or submit to elites.*

*Be polite,
at least
as much as possible.*

*Don't listen to them
if they say
"You have no future."*

*They are ignorant.
They only know
what old numbers say.*

*You choose your future.
Before you,
is the rough of life
you have to go through.*

*Let my words
be the tool you use
to carve the path
of your choosing.*

Far more uplifting than the other poems you've seen in here to this point, don't you agree?

Chapter 8

In October of 2016, I took the biggest leap of faith I could do. I moved out of my family home, and to my own apartment near Downtown Petoskey. I did it so I could be closer to work and my family wouldn't have to drive me to Petoskey everyday I work. I was without a vehicle at the time, so my primary means of getting places was walking. It was good exercise for the most part. But in hindsight my outer appearance may have been lacking for having to walk in all the elements. I do recall a few times I had to walk and I looked like crap upon arriving at the office.

The year 2017, I learned something that hit me harder than my realist mentality could ever hit me. My realist outlook and time have forced me to swallow my pride more times than I care to mention. Usually I can take it and continue on, but in this case, it knocked me to the ground and had me staggering to get up.

I felt alone one day in January and issued a social media challenge. I later wrote a poem about the final results of the challenge. Here is the poem that sums up everything. It's called "Post Challenge Shock".

Post Challenge Shock

When I felt alone,
I issued a birthday challenge on Facebook.

I was in shock.
It picked up faster
than I would have thought

I made the challenge at night on January 25, 2017,
I got a phone call on the next morning,
and a text message from old classmates.

After February 22, I had over
40 people wishing me well.

Combining the text messages, voice mails,
and the social media shout outs on the event page plus my
own profile,
it added up to be between 40 to 50 people telling me
what a good person I am and other positive impressions.

I was in awe.
I couldn't believe the response I got.

I realized, this whole time,
I was wrong.
I was blinded by my rage and anger
I held inside for so long.

It is a hard blow
when the truth is the opposite
of what you believe.

And shortly after the surprise wore off
I did a social media "thank you" and
admitted that I have been blind.
I never knew how blessed I have been.

It is possible that my old classmates may have been the way as I portrayed them. With the passing of time, people do change. I felt the way they thought of me in high school, still applied to that day. As the poem helped me admit, I was wrong.

I must also admit, if they did try to tell me that they cared, I wouldn't have believed them anyway. On the surface I would say, "Thank you", but inside my head I would think, "What are you up to?". I was blind to any sign of acceptance or acknowledgement back then. I saw and heard through the darkness I kept locked away. Even if all the proof was documented and laid out before me, I still wouldn't believe. I would say all of it was fabricated, none of it was real.

It is a hard hit when the original reason to push forward, to be better than everyone else, all those years turns out to be a lie you yourself made. But now, it doesn't matter. There is no changing the past, and I am stuck with the scars whether I like it or not. All I can do now is accept and admit I was wrong and keep going.

Chapter 9

Also in 2017, I did something I didn't think I would do. After talking to a counselor I have been seeing for a long time, he suggested I go to church. I rolled my eyes a bit and agreed. He told me to go to a "seeker church". In simpler terms, it's the type of church people who are looking to start their journey of faith go to.

I will admit, my first impression of the church when I went to the gathering location for the first time was "this is different". The gathering location was at the local high school and the service was in the school's auditorium. Genesis Church was a church without a physical base of operations. I never knew a church that didn't have a building of its own.

I learned quickly that a church is not a place, it is a people united by faith. Before every service, a team set everything up. And after the service, they packed everything up and made it look like they were never there come Monday morning. I never knew a church organization could be nomadic. At least these days I didn't think it was possible that a church could be nomadic.

The first Sunday of 2017 was my first day with Genesis Church. Feeling a bit out of place, I was sitting in a stand seating area close to the door. When they started playing the music, my first thought was "Dang, that's loud". Not only did I feel my ribcage shake, but I felt the seat in front of me vibrating. It was a subtle vibration, but I found it strange that the soundwaves were shaking chairs bolted to the floor.

I confess I liked the message they were conveying, but at the end of the first few services I attended I left. I power walked my way out of the school and back to my apartment. I knew my counselor would like me to attend at least four weeks worth of sermons before saying I was done. But I kept going because they were welcoming. After the music at the beginning and before the sermon started, they always gave a welcome statement. "Thank you for coming to Genesis Church. If this is your first time here, thank you for coming and we encourage you to keep coming." In those words more or less.

In the third or fourth week of attending, I opened up more. They had prayer teams available after each service. Easy concept, you walk up to one of the prayer teams and tell them what you could use prayer for and they would pray for you right there one person of the team at a time. Not many people took advantage of it. I was in a time of feeling lost and struggling. I thought to myself, "I got nothing to lose, and hopefully everything to gain". I went up to the stage where the prayer teams were and talked with them. I admitted I had darkness inside me I have been trying to get rid of. I didn't say anything about how bad it was. I didn't want to admit I had this darkness in me for over ten years and it was used as a driving force for me this whole time.

My first Easter service at Genesis, is one that I will never forget. It unfortunately wasn't because of the service message. It was because something happened to me. The best way to define what happened can be summed up in one term, spiritual warfare.

The meal of remembrance was beginning. They asked people to pray before getting in lines on the sides of the auditorium. I was sitting in a chair in the middle of the back row that goes across the whole auditorium. I bowed my head, clasped my hands together with my thumbs laying straight across my left index finger, with the nails of my thumbs against my forehead. I quietly said a prayer and said "Amen". I tried to lower my arms from the position I was praying in. My brain told my arms to move, but they didn't budge. Tried to lift my head, but it barely moved. It felt like my thumb nails were glued to my forehead. And my eyelids refused to open. I started to panic a little bit. Then a thought crossed my mind. I quietly recited an oath I was writing. An oath of service to the Lord. It was in poetry format at the time. Here is my oath of service.

Oath of Service

Dear LORD,

Forgive me,
for the sins I have done
and the shadows
that have grown
inside of me.

I beg
for forgiveness
for letting these shadows
linger inside me
for so long.

Help me be free
from the darkness.

In exchange,
I swear an oath.

Let this be
my oath of service.

I swear upon my life,
I will serve as a protector
of the people who praise you.
I will be the shield
that keeps them
safe from harm.

If those that attack
refuse to back down,
with a sense of regret
I will also be the sword
that strikes.

You teach to show compassion
to others, even those who wrong us.

In this state of madness
our world has fallen into,
I'm afraid I may have to be
the sword and the shield.

I will do my best
not be lethal.
All I will try to do
is defeat them.

If the shadows inside me
can not be removed.

After reciting those words, I tried to move my head. My head flew backward sending me from my slouched prayer position to the back of the seat I was sitting in. My hands dropped into my lap still clasped together. I took several deep breaths. I pulled my hands apart and it felt like my hands were sweating. I was scared, wondering what just happened. At that moment we were dismissed. As people started leaving, I walked out of the auditorium and went around a corner next to the doors. I thought "I got to talk to the pastor about this." I went to look for him in the auditorium. He wasn't there anymore. I walked out, probably with a mild look of panic on my face.

One of the church elders, E, walked up to me and said "Hey Ian, I saw you didn't take part in the meal, is everything alright?" I told him everything that happened. I told him how I couldn't move, my thumbs were stuck to my forehead, and after a deep prayer I was able to move again. His eyes grew a bit wide. After a few seconds he said " I think God is working in you. That's spiritual warfare. Would you mind if I pray over you?" My response was "Please do." I admit, I was scared at a level I couldn't recall ever being at before. He put his hand on my shoulder and prayed for me. I thanked him and headed back to the apartment.

I kept going to Genesis Church. Even though I think for most people, such an experience would scare them away from that religious establishment. What made me stay was the fact they actually cared. The staff, mostly volunteers, actually cared on a personal level about others in the church. And I'm not sure if there would have been anyone at any other church that would have offered support after me confessing to them that I felt complete paralysis during service.

Chapter 10

The year 2018, I made a decision that set me on a course that I am now grateful to be on. I decided to be Baptised. I told the lead pastor N, I was ready. It was April and the next official Baptism was in July when we would be doing outdoor services. The Baptism would be done in Little Traverse Bay.

Spring gave way to summer and July came soon enough. On July 8th 2018, I was next to Little Traverse Bay. The service was normal, then came toward the end of the service for baptism testimonies. I gave my testimony, along with a young man; I believe he was a high school student. I was baptised first. Pastor N asked me "Do you accept Jesus Christ as your Lord and Savior?" My answer was simple, "Yes."

"Ian, my brother, I baptise you in the holy spirit. Buried in the likeness of his death." Pastor N pushed me below the surface of Little Traverse Bay. I felt at peace while underwater at that moment. I wanted this feeling of peace to last forever. But it didn't last as long as I would have liked. I was pulled back to the surface, "Raised in the likeness of his resurrection," Pastor N said. The applause commenced as I surfaced and headed back to the shoreline.

I also started to serve the Lord another way. An old classmate of mine, M, recruited me to be a volunteer leader for a youth group organization called YoungLife. I ended up serving with the middle school part of the organization called WyldLife. It was fun for the most part. I was mostly the person behind the scenes getting stuff ready. I enjoyed being the person who got stuff ready. I volunteered for several years.

What I feel I did best were the Club talks. That's where I did a peep talk and read a bit of the Bible. The kids seemed to receive them very well. I admit, I did talks that made kids think or made them speechless.

I admit, even though I was serving the Lord, I wasn't growing spiritually. The darkness inside me was still there. It was slowly driving me insane. I did try telling it to go away in the name of Jesus. It didn't help most of the time.

I didn't know what to do. I thought being a humble servant of the Lord would help drive it out. I wasn't going to stop being a humble servant, but I felt defeated. The Lord still didn't abandon me.

One day leaving work, I got a call from M. She invited me to a bible study group her and her husband were having. I agreed to come. I figured I would give it a few sessions and see how it went. I walked over to the meeting location, which was the house M and her husband S were renting in Petoskey. It was supposed to start at 6:30 in the evening. But it usually got organized and underway when everyone arrived closer to 7. I was taught and trained by my parents that it's better to be early than late. So I showed up at their doorstep at 6:00.

I had no idea what they were to talk about. But this being my first time, I wasn't required to take part in the study discussion. I was required to do the reading for next time. They asked if anyone had prayer requests. I said I have a request, while quietly thinking, "if they are willing to help, great. If they immediately kicked me out, at least there were other things I could do on the nights they met.". I admitted I felt defeated and was dealing with darkness inside me.

After attending the group for a while S suggested going through a book called Bondage Breaker. He said he would read through it with me and we would discuss it when I arrived early for bible study. I agreed, because I had nothing to lose but everything to gain again. One chapter a week made the process take a number of months, but it was worth it.

The darkness was slowly losing its grip on me. Once I got to the point of exercises, there was a prayer/statement you were supposed to say out loud before each exercise. I did and on my walks to bible study after saying that, it was quiet in my head. No nagging thoughts, no negativity, just quiet. I admit I was very surprised. The darkness hasn't bothered me since I finished the exercises. And I am still going to that same bible study.

I made a deal with the Lord, and he delivered his end of the deal. The darkness doesn't have a hold on me. I call myself the Dark Wander that has been Redeemed. Here's a poem that talks about my spiritual journey.

Don't Let Me Fall

Sometimes everything is fine.
Sometimes everything is
as it always is inside.

Feeling at peace for the most part.
Then out of nowhere, BAM!

I fall spiritually face first

*on the path I been walking
and now I feel like I'm being dragged.*

*Not a slow drag,
like someone pulling me along.
I'm getting dragged backwards
at a speed of 15 to 20 miles an hour.*

*I then remember,
I still have a shackle on one leg
with a link of chain that keeps growing
as I keep moving forward.*

*I'm not being dragged to
Square One of my spiritual journey.
No, I'm getting dragged to the edge.*

*The edge that is a cliff
and down below
is a place I never want to be again.*

*Thankfully I stop
before my toes could go over
the edge between
salvation and damnation.*

*I get back on my feet.
Then suddenly
a jerk from the chain
knocks me off balance.*

*I'm right on the edge,
arms flailing, body shaking.*

I'm screaming,
I'm begging,
I'm praying,

"Please dear Lord
don't let me fall.

Don't left me fall back
into the darkness.

I can't go back.
I don't want to go back.
I'm not ready.

You saved me once,
no, you saved me more times than I can count.

You pulled me out after I spent
almost 15 years of my life in that.
I ran away from you
and used the power in that place
like a car uses gasoline.

I had to have more,
just to keep pushing forward.

Still you didn't abandon me,
you didn't forsake me.

When I finally got to the point
I couldn't do this anymore,
I couldn't pay the price.

You came down,

took my hand,
and guided me out.

Slowly but surely,
you got me out of there
and on this path back to you.

Now the Demons
are trying to pull me
back into the darkness.

Please dear Lord,
this humble servant needs you.
Please don't let me fall
back into the darkness."

The poem was written before being completely free. I do consider myself an addict in a sense. I never was one for drinking, smoking, or doing drugs. I was addicted to the power I got from the darkness. I used the strength I got from feelings of anger and rage as a personal motivation. There is no conventional rehab program for this addiction.

The most terrifying thought I have these days, is having to go into the darkness to save others. Even though I know others are struggling in the darkness as I was, and my selfless instincts tell me to go in and save others, I can't go into the darkness. Even to save those I care about, I can't go back into the darkness.

It's the same scenario with any addict. If they are offered what they were addicted to, there is a high probability of relapsing. If I go back into the darkness to save someone, there is a very high probability I'm not going to be able to get out again. And it doesn't help knowing that the chances of saving anyone is very slim after I go in to save them. To me, it's not worth the risk of losing myself.

Epilogue

Though the Lord has done so much for me over the years, I feel the least I can do is serve him faithfully. But he has blessed another way that I can't repay. He has given me the greatest gift I could ever ask for. I have been able to love and be loved in return.

I have struggled with my dating life, all my life. I never had a girlfriend. I was in my thirties and ready to give up. I felt I was living in a world that cares more about physical and outward appearances, than what is inside and the kind of person within. But the Lord blesses when we least expect it.

In 2019, I got a message from one of the online dating applications I had an account on. I was mildly surprised. With most online dating, any message I got was a mass send message or I sent the first message. When I got an email about getting a message on a dating app, my first thought was it was a mass email message. I checked it out to find it was a message addressed to me alone.

"This is new," I thought. We commenced to chat on the app for a good couple of days. The app gave a warning that the chat session would be automatically deleted after so long. We exchanged cell phone numbers. We continued to communicate off the service.

She is a good woman. It was a bit of a long distance relationship at first. I didn't have a car and she had no interest in driving. Eventually we were able to meet face to face in Gaylord Michigan. We agreed to meet at a coffee shop place. We met and went on to her favorite restaurant for dinner. Our first date was amazing. Good food, wonderful conversation at a booth table. Her parents did keep a slight eye on us in case anything weird happened or if she wanted to leave without me.

And for the first time that I can remember, I had a smile on my face without having to tell my face muscles to form one. After eating and talking, she called one of her parents over to take a picture of us together. She came over to my side of the table, and I put my left arm around her. With her, I finally knew what it was like to be happy. She loves me flaws and all.

In 2020 after the Michigan COVID lockdown, I went to Gaylord and put an engagement ring on her hand. I didn't get down on one knee and ask like you would do traditionally. I wrote a poem that did the talking for me and had her read it on my phone. While she was reading, I pulled out the ring.

In 2021, we became husband and wife. What makes her so perfect to me, is her mind and her heart. She makes me want to be a better Christian, and the size of her heart rivals my own. She is my greatest treasure, the love of my life. Until the Lord calls me home, I will love her with all of my heart.